Simple Formula for Successful Business/Church

This book is to provide information of the importance of how people should be treated and what I have learned, throughout my eighty-seven years and also many years within the business and church world.

First it is important we understand how to treat people. I list eighteen examples within my business career and personal life of successful ways I learned to best treat people.

These eighteen examples explain what is most important to be successful both in businesses and churches in their everyday life.

Copyright © 2019 by Ken Shores
Simple Formula for Successful Business/Church
Non-Fiction book by Ken Shores
Printed in the United States of America.
ISBN: 978-1-79470-338-4

All rights reserved solely by the author. The author guarantees all contents are original and do not infringe upon the legal rights of any other person or work. No part of this book may be reproduced in any form without the permission of the author. The views expressed in this book are not necessarily those of the publisher.

Dedication

It is an honor to dedicate this book first to God. Words are inadequate to express my thanks to Him, my loving and compassionate God. I also dedicate my writing to my loving Wife, Susan, my daughter Brenda and all the people I have had the pleasure to meet in my lifetime and to all who contributed to this book.

Previously Published Books By Ken Shores

1. Is There A God? How Do You Know?
2. Adventurous Life worth Living
3. A Donkey Christmas (1st Edition)
4. Donkey Christmas Story (2nd Edition)
5. I Spent Christmas with Jesus
6. Mystery in the Forest
7. Miracle Dream Teacher
8. Youth Restoring America
9. Mystery of the Bells
10. Simple Formula for Successful Business & Church
11. Can America be saved?
12. America History into Today
13. The Boy the Man and the Sea

<u>Available on Amazon, Facebook and soon on LuLu Publishing.</u>

<u>At the back of this book is summary of each book</u>

Important Information for each Example

------꽃CBSO꽃------

It is important to realize about the world we live in and what I use within, Includes the original oldest History book, in the world, the Bible, (Proven by the Dead Seas Scrolls). The Bible is my proof as my source to explain a short version used from the beginning of this earth being made.

This is the importance of all people as they play a major role in our world since their existence.

Since the beginning of this world when according to the Bible, was created because of Lucifer, the head Angel challenged God his creator, that he was more than equal to God.

History of Lucifer/Satan – Who is he?

Satan is often caricatured as a red-horned, trident-raising cartoon villain; no wonder people question the history of Satan.

His existence, however, is not based on fantasy. It's verified in the same book that narrates Jesus' life and death **(Genesis 3:1-16, Isaiah 14:12-15; Ezekiel 28:12-19; Matthew**

4:1-11).
Christians believe Satan acts as leader of the fallen angels. These demons, existing in the invisible spirit realm yet affecting our physical world, rebelled against God, but are ultimately under God's control.

Satan masquerades as an "angel of light," deceiving humans just as he deceived Eve in very beginning **(Genesis 3)**.

Jesus Himself testified of Satan's existence. During His ministry, He personally faced temptation from the devil **(Matthew 4:1-11)**, casting out demons possessing people **(Luke 8:27-33)**, and defeated the evil one and his legion of demon angels at the cross.

Christ also helped us understand the ongoing, spiritual war between God and Satan, good and evil **(Isaiah 14:12-15; Luke 10:17-20)**.   With Jesus Christ on our side, we need not fear Satan's limited power **(Hebrews 2:14-15)**. We ought to be wise, however, in resisting his tactics: You will find my examples used some of the Bible to make it workable.

The key to choices people make will determine their future. Satan made the worst choice that could have ever been made when challenging God. Now each of us are faced with our choices to be made also.

Successes and failures in this world today is depended on the choices we make. If we do not take the responsibility to determine who we accept and who we reject, then we have avoided making choices and may suffer later for not making choices. We make choices of where we are going to live, if we are going to church and which one, also for family etc.

In the business & church world when choosing people, we must determine in choosing each person if it will help them to be successful. This is the reason this book is being written, is to make the reader aware that every single person we work with and our friendship must be evaluated and always do this in a friendly way.

The more we know about the people in our business & church surroundings, then this promotes a better business & church world. Remember that choice began with God and Satan before this world was created. In this book I have written my experiences with choice in the Business & church world to alert you to the importance of choices being made.

Eighteen examples of the Simple Formula

------ఈుఁఔఁ ------

<u>Have you checked to why many companies and Churches fail to succeed after a few years in business?</u>

Some companies and churches suddenly after many years in business also start their journey to failure. In this book, you might be surprised, as to one very important reason for failure that is covered and with possible solutions.

In my many years in the business world from worker to upper management, plus owning my own businesses I have learned many reasons for failure.

Sharing my experience with you the reader will have many answers to how you can avoid loss of business and or church. I am 87 years old, traveled over most of the world and have 45 years of education; I served in the Army from November 1949 until January 1953. Graduated from Fort Sam Houston Military Medical School as a Surgical Technician.

Station in Free Territory of Trieste from July 1950 to December 1952 and discharged January 1953. Also, I am a Disabled Veteran.

I am currently featured in the 2017 Strathmore's Who's Who Worldwide as Professional of the Year.

I have worked for large Corporations, owned several businesses and belong to several organizations. I served on the Board of Directors and Board of Trustees of People to People International (Created by President Eisenhower) for several years and was in charge of groups traveling to different places throughout the world.

I am still involved with Lake Pointe Baptist Church (Rockwall TX) since 1980, where I have served as Youth Director, Youth Teacher, In charge of ushers, Story Teller and Youth Play Writer.

Additional information about my life is in my published books, "Is There a God? How Do You Know" and "Adventurous Life worth Living" available in Amazon and LuLu Publishing.

(Example 1)

I was discharged in 1953, from the Army and I purchased a used car in Muncie Indiana, from a dealer, setting up a payment plan. After having the car for a few weeks, the payment clerk stopped on a Sunday and asked if I could make my monthly payment as Sunday was the last day of the month.

He stated this would help his bookkeeping for month end. I agreed and made the payment. A few days later I mention to my uncle about making the car payment on Sunday. My uncle explained to me my car is now paid for and tomorrow he will take me to Indianapolis because at that time in Indiana any payment received on Sunday for a payment plan is considered payment in full.

The next day I found my car was debt free and the dealer must give me a clear title. This kind of business mistake can bankrupt the company.

Make sure you always know the rules and regulations of whatever you are doing with other people.

(Example 2)

In 1957 I began working at Griffin Wheel Company in Chicago as Manager of the Warehouse and the outside yard. The yard Forman and his employees were under my supervision.

One major job was unloading train freight cars of 100 lbs. Bags of white sand used in production of pouring steel. The unloading took three days per freight car.

I told my yard Forman I had received permission to make a special offer to him and the four men that unloaded the freight cars. That the next car to be unloaded today, if it could be unloaded in one day, him and the other four men will get the next day off with pay.

The freight car was unloaded that day, and the Forman and the four employees became thankful employees. My boss told me what a great way to save the company money and also create employee relationship.

In 1958 the President of Griffin Wheel Company called me in for a meeting. My boss and the President told me that Griffin Wheel is building a new plant in, near Kansas City. I was offered the job as Plant Office Manager, and I will be given all the plans to make sure the plant was built as designed.

I agreed, and my wife and one child was given an expense account that included moving and house rental. We moved and rented a house. After the first month, I was introduced to the Chairman of the Board's son who was appointed as the Vice President over me. Within the first week, he made changes in the building plan that could not work for this new plant.

He told me that he is in charge and I was not to question his changes. He continued to tell me, his mother is Chairman of the Board, and I must follow his leadership. I realized I would be blamed for his mistakes and called the President.

The President agreed but told me that he tried to stop the Chairman of the Board from having her son taking over being in charge. He also said several times this man has messed up their business. I told him if he is staying I would resign and find another job.

I left the company and opened a Restaurant that was successful. I learned later that Griffin wheel lost a large sum of money and finally they were able to fire the Vice president for all his mistakes.

Businesses, to be successful, and must be sure all employees are working as required and well chosen.

(Example 3)

In 1959 we moved back to Chicago. Being I graduated from Northwestern Business College and majored in Business Accounting went to work at Motorola. I was hired as an Accountant Manager.

Within a few months I was offered a new job. Motorola like other businesses were using the large IBM Computers for Payroll only. Being Motorola shipped equipment to many places in the world, decided to work a plan to use the IBM computers to take care of orders and shipping.

To do this, it would require people to assist designing programs to handle this process. I was selected to be on the team to work with **Argonne National Laboratory, International Harvester, IBM and Motorola.**

In the business world, this was the first time computers started to be used for more than Payroll. I was on the designing Team and we all went to school at the IBM Institute in Chicago first.

When we had completed the design with IBM for the new system, I was assigned as Manager of card keypunch for tracking equipment shipping overseas. The Motorola

Payroll keypunch cards were also included. I had my own office, (on the Executive floor) and a secretary, plus six women keypunch operators.

When I first started, I set up at lunchtime a table for all of us to enjoy lunch together. This way during this time we associated as a family. Our production was the best in Motorola and my boss, a Vice President congratulated me on our work. He also had me write up how I was able to establish a team of employees that were so productive.

The results were that Motorola met with managers and supervisors to also use this type plan for their employees. The important part to remember is when people feel like that they are treated like a family member, then their working habits improve for the benefit of the company. Also gives them a better chance for advancement.

In 1963, I was offered a chance to work in Motorola Production Engineering, so I could train to take over the position as an Electrical Engineer when a new plant in Elgin, Illinois opened.

This was the year we bought our first home in Glendale Heights, Illinois. During the two years,

I was in Production Engineering, and our department was like a close-knit family—from the vice-president down to all of the employees. After-hours, social events were scheduled several times a month which included our spouses. We enjoyed parties, square dancing, hayrides and more.

One of the saddest days in America's history was witnessed by all of us on televisions we had been testing. The networks showed the people of Dallas as they lined the streets to catch a glimpse of President John F. Kennedy on Friday, November 22, 1963.

We watched in horror as the shots that was heard around the world rang out killing our President and wounding Texas Governor Connelly. All work stopped immediately!

(Example 4)

A few days later, I faced a major challenge at work when the director assigned me to coordinate some production changes done by the Development Engineering Department. I was to have the Final Assembly Television Foreman incorporate those changes promptly. My fellow employees explained to me that Dick, the Foreman, was a very hard man to convince that the required changes are to be implemented. Besides that, his mother was one of Motorola's largest stockholders, and she was the Vice Chairman on the Board of Directors.

I received the exact changes on a Television Model, that were to be made, and my instructions were to have them installed as soon as possible.

With the knowledge of the difficulty I would probably experience confronting the foreman, I decided to use 'The Negative Approach' I had learned from a door-to-door salesman. I rolled out a cart that had a covered prototype of the changes to be made.

As I approached the foreman, I said to him. "I have something you may be…OH NEVER MIND," and started walking away. He immediately ran after me and told me to finish what I was saying to him. I replied, "I know you're busy and just wanted to wait until you had some time."

His curiosity was aroused, and he said, "That's okay. I will make time for you now." I then explained how someone is always trying to make changes, and I just wanted his opinion. I told him I would wait for a more convenient time. With that, I again turned around and started walking away.

This time, he ran until he was standing in front of the cart and said, "Ken, its OKAY! I have time now," in an almost begging voice. I told him, "If you are sure you have time, I will show you these dumb changes they came up with this time."

With that, I took off the cover and showed him the prototype. He looked at it, and after examining each of the changes that was to be made. He told me, "These changes are to be made as soon as we can get a break in the production line."

I told him I was glad someone like him looked at this, and I respect your opinion. He even took me to the production line to explain how the changes were going to be incorporated. When I walked back into Production Engineering, several were applauding me and telling me to share my secret of how I was able to have Dick make the changes without a fight. I gladly shared my approach and how it reminded me of Proverbs 4:7: "The beginning of wisdom is this: Get wisdom. Though it cost all you have, get understanding".

I used wisdom I had received from previous training, and it gave me the insight and understanding necessary to deal with a difficult situation. This was because I was told, I would need to use creativeness to convince a boss who was not easily persuaded.

I not only used a tactic I had learned from my past experiences, but I wanted it to appear that the boss had come up with the idea. It was refreshing to see God at work in our office, and we all cared about each other, just like the Bible says we are supposed to. Many wonderful stories of God putting the right people in the right place at the right time are of my fondest memories. This is another example of how to encourage people to work better at their job.

A few months later our Manager, John Biga called me into his office and said that Motorola has canceled building a plant in Elgin and I will transferred back to the International division in the Executive offices. You will be on the Executive Payroll and working with International customers and International Divisions.

I was moved into an Executive office with an Executive desk and, was placed on the Executive payroll. My job was to work with people from other countries and also take them out to dinner at Motorola's expense. Data Processing was still included with this position.

(Example 5)

One late evening I was working in my office when a Vice President came in. Without saying a word he hit my heavy executive desk with his fist so hard it jumped off the floor. Then he apologized, and said, everything is going wrong and I need someone to talk to about it. After he explained his problems, I made some suggestions and he said; he couldn't thank me enough for listening to me and for my suggestions. We both closed up our offices and walked out together. This is another example of people working together for your company and can help one another.

My last transfer was to the Frank Kaplan team, before leaving Motorola in 1978. I will now include in summarizing by using what I had learned also from Frank Kaplan at Motorola when I was assigned to be a member of his team. Motorola wasn't aware of any interviews I was having from companies wanting to hire me.

The Motorola Board of Directors had hired a person in 1975, by the name of Frank Kaplan. He had just completed his contract with John Deere and saved them from dissolving the company.

During World War II Mr. Kaplin was assigned to help all war assembly plants to motivate the employees the importance of their job to provide what is needed for America to be saved from the war.

During Mr. Kaplan's first six months, no one knew he had been hired to devise a plan to keep Motorola not only profitable but a respected company. In his first week he spoke to all the Motorola Communications Division employees, including all management, including from the President down, in several large scheduled meetings. He outlined the past and present structures of Motorola's operations philosophy and then sketched out the possibilities of the future.

(Example 6)

One illustration he shared was how important each employee was to the success of the company. He used the example of a multimillion-dollar contract that was to be delivered to a country's government with some communications equipment for wireless telephones because of the many mountains, and was to be completed within a certain time frame. One of the most import parts of the equipment was a special transmitting tube that took six months to make.

He then said, could you imagine the importance if the project was in the final stages of completion with only the transmitting tube to be installed for the final testing, and the project was ten days ahead of schedule? Then the assembly manager personally was to carry the tube to the area of the final testing so it could be installed.

He didn't see the trash on the floor in a supposedly clean area and tripped. The tube broke, which would cause Motorola to lose their multimillion-dollar contract. What the assembly manager didn't know was the trash hadn't been picked up by the janitor that day because he'd fought with his wife before leaving for work.

Mr. Kaplan continued to explain that even what happens to people outside of work is important to a company and its success. All management must be trained to have respect and consideration for all employees no matter who they report to. Mr. Kaplan also told everyone this could be a possibility of happening when that tube is received and ready to be shipped within the next few weeks.

Frank Kaplan planned to choose the best employees within their field to make up a team of seven, and I was one chosen for the field from data processing.

We as a team learned much from Mr. Kaplan who had been contracting with companies since World War II. His job was to investigate how they can be successful. What I respected most was that the principals and ideas he proposed we learned had been taken from the Bible.

It was an honor to work for such a man who taught us that the most important thing to learn in life is to have respect for yourself and all the people around you.

For the next two years, I was part of the team chosen by Mr. Kaplan and on assignment using the computer to develop systems to help improve Motorola's way of doing business. During this time, each of us used our expertise in different fields, and it made us a great team that was effective in many areas.

(Example 7)

I had an unusual thing happen with another team member. I walked into a mathematician's office and looked at his blackboard full of writing. He had a Ph.D., and I didn't understand anything he had written. He said that what I was looking at was a very complex problem, and it was driving him crazy trying to find the answer.

I told him that even though nothing on the board made any sense to me, I have solved complex problems within Data Processing that were effective in the programming department and our system design.

I walked him through the steps I used to teach others. Even without knowing the meaning of what we were looking at, he followed my procedure, and it helped him come up with a solution. He thanked me and said, "It's simple to solve things now with the procedure you taught me." As a team, we learned from each other.

Learning best how to understand people.

Shortly after our team was organized, Frank Kaplan called all of our team together and announce that all Vice-presidents, Top General Managers of some departments and the President of Motorola will each be giving a presentation to us about their positions and how they communicate with their people in two weeks. The presentations will begin at 4 PM and be completed by 6:00 PM. At 6:30 all of us will join together for supper and a time to visit with each other.

The purpose of this event is to determine how we can make changes to do better jobs that will benefit Motorola and all employees. Mr. Kaplan also told us not to speak to anyone about any business matters until we meet for supper. He also told us that within the next three days he will explain to the team their part in this presentation and also at the meal and afterward at the Get Acquainted meeting.

Three days later the team learned that only Frank Kaplan will be asking questions during each presentation and we are to remain silent. He also quoted Bible scripture **"Matthew 22:37-39 & Leviticus 19:18 New International Version (NIV) ^{37} Jesus replied: "'Love the Lord your God with all your heart and with all your soul and with all your mind.' ^{38} This is the first and greatest commandment. ^{39} And the second is** like it: 'Love your neighbor as yourself", Leviticus 18:18 Do not seek revenge or bear a grudge against anyone among your people, but love your neighbor as yourself. I am the LORD.** This tells us that God has instructed each of us of how we are to treat all people.

In the business or church world, everyone should think of everyone else as their neighbor. If a person doesn't live up to being a good neighbor, then that person needs to be moved either to a different place in the company or let go from the company.

Before the day of the presentation, Frank Kaplan spent several hours with the team rehearsing what we were to do after the presentation during the meal and getting to gather with upper management. We learned how best to speak to them and how to ask questions. Each person was assigned who they should talk to after the meal. Frank Kaplan had worked with President Bob Galvin, the President to establish this Presentation as to what executive were to talk about.

Note: *I first meet Bob Galvin personally, when I was Manager of Key Punch. One day I had a* *full box of Payroll keypunched cards, and on the second landing of stairs, Bob Galvin was rushing up the stairs, hit my arm and cards went everywhere. He apologized, then helped me put all the cards back into the box. He asked my name and what department I worked in. I told him my title and thanked him for all his help. My boss, a Vice-President told me later that Bob Galvin told him how he met me and I must be a good Manager. Bob Galvin was a very kind likable person.*

When the presentation began, the Motorola President was the first person to speak. President Bob Galvin introduced each of us and why we were attending the presentation. Then he introduced the Executive Vice President and said he will begin this Presentation Program.

(Example 8)

The Executive Vice President first told us about himself and then began explaining the various departments he was responsible for and how many employees were involved. He named the Vice-Presidents, Managers and the Supervisors who reported to him.

Frank Kaplan interrupted and asked how many of the total employees, including Vice-Presidents, Managers and Supervisors, has he met personally. He replied the Vice-Presidents, Managers and most of the Supervisors at our staff meeting. Only a few of the rest of my employees.

Mr. Kaplan thanked him and said you can continue. After the Executive Vice president gave a brief description of his departments he was responsible for, Mr. Kaplan again interrupted and asked what kind of reports do you receive to keep you informed of all your employees working conditions?

The Executive Vice-President answered, I receive a monthly report from my Managers and sometimes additional reports if problems arise.

Mr. Kaplan then asked, do you receive reports from your supervisors?

He replied, sometimes at our Staff Meetings. Again Mr. Kaplan thanked him and said to continue. The Executive Vice president completed his presentation in a few minutes by giving a brief detail about what is his responsibilities.

Then Mr. Kaplan said he had three more questions. First, out of all the many employees you have can you be sure each person is performing their job for the benefit of Motorola? He answered I feel we have a good system and all our employees are a credit to Motorola.

Question two, if you found out that some of your employees were making their own profit and taking advantage of Motorola, how would you take care of this action?

He answered, I would call immediately for an emergency staff meeting. I would then explain what I found out some employees are taking advantage of Motorola and have my Managers and Supervisors investigate all departments for who is responsible.

Mr. Kaplan interrupted and asked, what if some of you managers and Supervisors are managing this profit taking?

The Executive Vice-President replied, if no one reported any problem I would appoint an investigating team from our security department to find answers to who is responsible for this criminal activity to make immediate charges against the people responsible. Then Mr. Kaplan said this could take weeks in this process and Motorola could lose a great sum of money. I want to take a couple of minutes to talk to you in private.

(Example 9)

After the private meeting. The Executive Vice-President said I want to thank you, Mr. Kaplan, for your advice. I now will revise our system after talking to Mr. Kaplan. First will establish programs that during the year to meet all of the people from time to time that are working in the departments that are under my responsibility. This will included also having special gathering away from work which includes families that are also invited. This way we can all help one another when needed at work and away from work. This will also reduce the chance of anyone taking advantage of Motorola to illegally steal from Motorola.

Mr. Kaplan then thanked him for his presentation, and we will summarize all presentations when everyone has completed their presentation.

All presentations were very similar to the Executive Vice President's with the same type questions asked by Frank Kaplan and very similar answers. The President, Bob Galvin again spoke as the last person to speak. He first thanked all of his Executives for their presentations and for all the time and effort to prepare for this event as directed. Then he also thanked Frank Kaplan and his team for being here to make Motorola a good family company. He explained that we hired Frank Kaplan to help us like he did John Deere and many other companies to succeed. Motorola was not in as bad shape as John Deere but wanted him to help us to avoid getting into that position. His first day here we had all people employed by Motorola to hear Frank Kaplan's opening talk about how important every employee is to the success of the company. We heard him speak about a major project we were working on for another country and how one employee could have cost Motorola many thousands of dollars and lose the contract. Frank Kaplan will now continue with this presentation with a summarization based on your answers to his questions. Mr. Kaplan the floor is yours.

(Example 10)

Thank you, President Galvin and all you executives and Managers for each of your presentations. I also, want to thank each of my team for being here also. After our dinner we will take some time to meet each other. My team will also assist in getting to know you better. Now in the summarization of the presentation, each of you are wondering why I asked almost the same type questions and why were they asked.

In my many years of working with companies to make them more successful, I found first God in the Bible gave us a guideline as how important each person is. This same thing I told my Team that I now will tell you. In the Bible in **"Matthew 22:37-39 New International Version (NIV) 37 Jesus replied: "'Love the Lord your God with all your heart and with all your soul and with all your mind.'[a] 38 This is the first and greatest commandment. 39 And the second is like it: 'Love your neighbor as yourself", Leviticus 18:18 Do not seek revenge or bear a grudge against anyone among your people, but love your neighbor as yourself, I am the LORD.**

This told us that God has instructed each of us of how we are to treat all people. In the business world, everyone in any company should think of everyone else in the company as their neighbor. If a person doesn't live up to being a good neighbor, then that person needs to be moved either to a different place in the company or let go.

Now let us evaluate the questions I asked each of you, do we know all of our employees well enough to avoid what I first said to everyone that attended my first meeting with a possibility of a major problem. This was about the floor sweeper that had a fight with his wife that would cause Motorola to lose a large sum of money. Now I ask each of you is your system such that you can feel sure you know each of your employees well enough to avoid most problems that could be caused within Motorola.

Can you feel satisfied that today Motorola has not lost any business or money due to your employees? The most important reason for me to be assisting companies is to first work with the people in charge to help them solve any possible problems they may have. You will find that many times people are working in the wrong line of work and it could help them and the company if they moved to where they are more qualified to be. If you know of a person that is well liked by other people and if that person is working on a production line, then that person may be of more benefit by being in charge of that production line.

My job is to provide a system for each of you to be able to know your employees. As a starter, I gave you an example within Motorola. Also, management needs to take some time to send recognition to employees that have been brought to your attention of how great of a job they are doing. Make sure you sign what you send and also have it publicized with the company. Other employees will take notice and try to improve their working for the company.

(Example 11)

John Biga's mother is on the Board of Directors, and he is the Manager of the Production Engineering. That department is a close net family type department within Motorola. The employees and bosses have various times after work, get together and become better known together when their families become involved away from work. Cook-outs, dinners, events, etc. are planned and employees, including their families are invited. This way working together they all help one another.

This is only one of many examples we will explore in order to make Motorola a family company. I also again thank your Executive Vice President for taking my advice and working on ways to better know all of his employees. Now we can adjourn for our supper and getting to know each other.

(Please note; the actual details of how Frank Kaplan asked question was not complete as stated. Frank Kaplan had a way by asking questions to each Executive that made them look like a bad person in their job, then followed up

with asking questions that make that person to be a well-liked hero for Motorola. Mr. Kaplan had a way with words like I have never heard before that made you have the greatest respect for him and his knowledge. For the two years I worked as a team member, I learned more from Frank Kaplan than anyone else, and that has helped me many times throughout my life.)

During the last six months at Motorola in 1978, I continued to have interviews during my lunch time and week-ends, with a company who previously had been talking to me about joining their company, plus other companies also.

I will continue to take you through some of the challenges I have been involved with as to problems within the business world. Until 1975 I did not recognize some of the simple solutions that can keep businesses out of trouble.

In 1978 I left Motorola and went to work at E-Systems Inc. in Greenville Texas, and this was after many interviews with many companies that were interested in hiring me. E-Systems was interested in my background with computers and computer programming. Also, that I was leaving Motorola working in upper management. Within two months my Top Clearance Security was approved because I had it approved when I was in the Army. This was a completely different environment of my previous employment and even with people being friendly. There were some company family type employees.

In 1979 I was transferred to the Garland Texas Division, where there were much more family-friendly employees.

There were special events for employee families to also be involved. Because of all their business was all Government work it was also very secure about what we talked about. The Garland Division used the Greenville computers through wireless communications.

I was transferred as the Data Processing Manager in charge of installing the first internet communications throughout the Garland Division. New IBM Commercial Computers were also installed. The friendly relationship atmosphere between employees was a big benefit to the company.

(Example 12)

Another example of how careful in management you must be with what you say happened when all the equipment was installed. Trudy was the Manager in charge of installing the IBM Computers. When the installation was completed, she made the statement that these computers are so secure that no one can interfere with their processing.

In that same meeting, I told her that there are ways that can happen where security may fail. She insisted that her statement was correct. I told her I am not a betting man but willing to bet $100 that I could stop her computers. Several people that know my background talked to her and she changed her statement to "she has done everything possible to avoid problems". What she did not know that being I was in charge of the network and that I have the knowledge how to take a connection into the computer to break the security codes. If I made a special coil and connected it to the computer with a special rod moving it would find codes to enter into the computer. Then the computer would stop working correctly. Always be careful what you say and how you challenge anyone.

(Example 13)

Also during the time, I was working for the Garland Division of E-Systems, in 1980 a new Baptist Church, named Dalrock Baptist Church opened its new church building. My wife, family and I attended their first service in their new building. The church building held less than one hundred people. Before opening the new building, they met in a Bait House by the Lake.

When Pastor Steve Stroope finished his sermon, he asked for volunteers to help remove the hallway wall to add more space for people attending the church, as the church was overcrowded the first Sunday. I was one of those volunteers after work. It was great to see friendly people work together to help a church. Within a few weeks, I was assigned to join another person as an adult Sunday School Teacher. We became friends and now are very good friends.

As in the business world, most of the people of the church became volunteers. Their friendship grew quickly with the Wednesday night supper. By the friendship of one and another the church soon outgrown the first part of the church and a second part was added on.

By this kind of friendship, working people also developed more friendship at their place of work. Later the church in its continued growth changed its name to Lake Pointe Church and today now is among the largest churches in the United States. This is an excellent example for businesses to better understand the importance that all people should be considered important and when friendship is developed, it will also help businesses to be successful.

Another example I will share is when I became involved with the church, I also took on positions that were assigned to me. Not only did I share teaching with adults, at the request of the Pastor, I became Youth Director, Youth Teacher, Youth Story Teller and Youth Play Writer, plus headed up the ushers over several years at this church. The importance to Businesses and the church, is friendship and is important to success.

(Example 14)

After several weeks attending church in the men's class I attended, we had a new person join us. Even after welcome him he said you people don't want a person like me in your class. I am a terrible sinner and don't get along with people. The men shocked him when we all said together we are all sinners and we are here to help one another. He then said he was a roofer and we all have a habit of using bad language. We then started shaking his hand and told him we are here for the friendship and to help each other to change to a better life. He then sat down and listen to the lesson from the teacher. His wife asked me in the church service, what did you do to my husband as he has been avoiding going to church as he thought it was a waste of time. Now he said he enjoyed the class. And because this man mention in class he didn't have a Bible and wouldn't waste his money on buying one. Myself and a friend that afternoon went over to this man's house and presented him with a Bible and also spent some time with him and his wife. They both thanked us and they both for the first time, joined a church. How you treat people can lead into friendship.

(Example 15)

Later at the church I became Youth Director and Youth Sunday School Teacher. One class I taught I was informed that three boys were being added to my class and are friends with each other. I also was told to watch them closely as they are known as trouble makers. One is the son of the Music Minster and the other two are sons of Sunday teachers. On their first day setting at the back of the class, they began talking to each other.

This was disturbing our class, and I pointed my finger at them and told them wait until after class to talk. A short time later the boys again started talking. This time I said nothing and wrote each of their names on the blackboard. One of the boys asked why I did that.

I told them you will find out and continued with teaching the class. A little later they again started talking. This time I put a check mark by each name. By the time I had three check marks, I had no more problems with the three boys. I never told them why, and for all the rest of the classes had no more problems. They also showed respect to me and others for the rest of the year.

When people do not know why they are being corrected when they know they are wrong, they are more likely to show respect to you depending on the action you take.

(Example 16)

When I retired from work I started some of my own businesses. We also were raising a Granddaughter. When she was a teenager, and in high school, she was invited to travel to Russia with a group selected by People to People International.

I then started being involved and started a local chapter in the Dallas area. The parents of the other teenagers traveling to Russia were also involved in this chapter. I started Banquets, Student Ambassador of the Year program, etc. Students were invited on radio shows, meeting with Mayors, Governors, and other officials. After four years I was voted on to the Board of Directors.

For more than six years I led adult groups to countries all over the world. Thru all this time again it showed the importance of friendship and togetherness. I will share a few more examples of how important friendship can be.

In my talks to Student Ambassadors before they made their trip to another country, I talked to them about the importance of friendship. I started by first asking them to give me the name of their favorite book. After hearing the title names, then I picked out a Student Ambassador and asked for their title again. I then asked, did the book cover with title help you pick out that book.

The answer always came back as yes. Then asked if the cover looked bad to you, would you have gotten that book to read, even if you liked the title. The answer was always no. If the cover looked bad to you then you would not have ever read your favorite book.

I then said I look at a person from the inside out and never judge a person by their looks. The way a person or book looks from the outside does not mean that this is how you should judge them. The color of their skin and their outward appearances could keep you from finding your best friend.

(Example 17)

On a trip I lead for People to People International to Africa, we learned again, how important it is on how you treat people. The driver of our vehicle lived in a Muslim territory. He and his family were strong Christians. He told us that one day when he, his wife and four children were sitting down to eat, there was a knock on the door. When he open the door, four large men pushed the door open and grabbed him. For quite a while in front of his family, they were beating him up saying how dare you live here as a Christian. Then when the four men were about to leave, he told them that they were just about to have dinner and would you like to join us?

The four men were shocked and join them for dinner. He then told us that these four men left, as good friends. The lady riding with him up front asked, how you could do that! He answered; this is what it says in the Bible to love your enemies.

When we arrived at the place, we would spend two days at, all if the groups gather together before supper. This driver was asked to share his story with the whole group.

Everyone benefited from hearing about following the Bible of how we are to treat people. We all wondered if we could forgive someone like the driver did after being treated the way he was.

(Example 18)

On the fifth day of one of my People to People International, Mission in Understanding trip to Greece, and other countries. On our flight to Greece, I sat next to a man when we talked, made it clear he was an Atheist. He and his family lived in Hawaii, and he had been a successful surgeon who was now retired. He said it was a waste of time for me and my family to be involved with religion believing in a non-existing God. He asked why I wasted my time with such foolishness.

I explained in detail why I knew there is a loving God and how He has revealed Himself to me many ways. I used examples from the Bible, but he didn't seem to be impressed.

I was the leader, and a member of the delegation and four days later this same man asked if he and I could have supper together away from the group. It was a free night for all of us, and I didn't want to go shopping with my wife or other members of the delegation, so I said yes.

Then, at the restaurant, half-way through our conversation, he told me his daughter and son who is along with his wife had never had to be concerned regarding religion or God. They all led a very wonderful, successful life with no problems. He continued that his son was also a very successful surgeon following in his father's footsteps and his daughter was successful lawyer as well.

I asked him, "During your many years of marriage and raising two children, were there disagreements or any doubt about who you are or what the future held for you and your family?" He admitted that since I had put it that way, he had to be honest and tell me there were many times questions came to mind which he didn't have any answers that made sense. I next asked him, "Do you love your wife and children?" He acted as though he was almost shocked, but answered, "Of course I do!" Then I asked, "What is love and how can you explain it?" He said, "You got me there."

"This is something within yourself, and you know how you feel towards someone. The surgeon then asked me to explain the 'three Gods in one' that is in your Bible. I first asked him, "Is there a difference in how you feel when you are happy and full of love, or angry and hurt? Or depressed and want to give up?" He answered,

"Yes, naturally."

"You could compare three persons in one as having different roles of how you think and feel based on those three conditions. In our Bible, it talks about the Father, Son, and Holy Ghost, with God the Father overseeing everything. The Son experienced life as a perfect person, died to defeat death, and the Holy Ghost dwells in each of us that accept God's free gift of faith in His Son, Jesus Christ. Overall, they are one with three different roles, but beyond that, only God could explain why man who has never physically seen God on earth could never understand until sin was removed." You repeated several times, 'If you can't prove something it is not real, but must has a logical answer.' When you see a clear sky, can you explain why it's blue or where storms and other disasters really come from? What about the air you breathe? Do you see it and what is the whole answer to this? As a surgeon, you've dealt with women and childbirth. Have you figured out where it all really started?" "I get your point," he told me.

"I believe that God exists, and the only way to have eternal life with Him is to believe in His Son, Jesus. The Bible, God's Word, is the road map of life we are taught to follow. If I am wrong, I have led a good life that I can be proud of regardless of whether God really exists or not. If you are wrong, you will you spend eternity in the fire's pits of hell, and I will spend eternity in paradise. Instead of answering my questions he said,

"I can't shake your faith can I?" I told him, no, but I said to him, "I love you as a brother because of what Jesus taught, no matter what. I still believe God made each of us, and we each have a purpose in life." He said, "I see we have spent three hours talking, and I enjoyed being with you, but now for the first time in my life, I am totally confused." I told him maybe he should check it out for himself about what we talked about.

On our tenth day in Greece, we arrived at the Greek Island Patmos and visited the Monastery above the cave where Saint John wrote Revelation. It was rich with religious history. Then we were scheduled to tour the cave below the Monastery where John wrote Revelations. When we approached the stairway going down to the cave, I noticed a long line as far as I could see of people waiting to visit the cave. Our tour guide walked over to the person in charge, and he inserted our group at the top of the stairs. Our tour guide explained to us that most of the time, a long line of people from all over the world wait for hours to visit the cave. We were told that the stairway was steep, and a long way down to the cave's entrance. Also, we were told no pictures were allowed to be taken inside the cave, and we must be careful not to touch anything. No talking was allowed after entering, and so I waited by the door to make sure our entire group was there. The retired Surgeon was one of the last of our group, and he stopped at the entrance. I told him to go ahead, and he told me he couldn't go any further. I explained to him this is a once in a lifetime opportunity to see something like this. But he explained he couldn't explain why, but for some reason, there was no way he could enter the cave. I mentioned to him that he said nothing ever bothers him, and he replied, "There is no way I can enter this cave." I told him if he changed his mind, we would wait for him by the stairway. Once I entered the cave, I realized I was in a very special place and seemed to feel God's presence all around me.

It was much larger than I expected with painting on the walls and plaques with explanations of different areas. When completing my tour, I found the Atheist standing at the entrance staring at what was written above the door. He told me again he couldn't explain why he could not enter the cave but knew somehow not to go in.

I still wondered if it was the devil or God that kept him out of this meaningful experience. He did write me several times when we got home; I leave it to God for final results.

(This Example is taken from my life story book) "is there a god? How do you know" and "ADVENTUROUS LIFE WORTH LIVING,"(2nd Editon woth differen title) that is about my life, available in Amazon, LuLu Publishing, Barnes & Noble plus more

These are pictures of the cave mentioned

The Castle of Patmos shown above has the Cave of Apocolyse underneath it. The building houses several Monasteries and a museum.

Cave of Apocolype on Patmos, Island was were it is said John wrote the book of Revelation. The photo to the *right* is a larger picture of what everyone saw above the door as they entered the cave.

These 18 examples are to show the importance of how we treat people will determine the success of business and churches and the life we live.

Each person is responsible for themselves and how they treat people. In the business world, the people chosen by a business will play a major role to keep a business successful. This also applies to Churches, Organizations, and Government to their success.

If the staff and the heads of a church, organization, and government do not perform in accordance for what it stands for, the church, organization or government will fail because of chosen people. In the business and church world, each person must be evaluated to determine if they are contributing to the success of the business and church. If you have people that are in good spirits and enjoy their position, then the first step is in favor of the business and church or place that they are responsible for. Then proceed to continue to evaluate people. If a person does not meet the standards of the first step, find out why and what it would take to correct it if possible.

Set up your standards and procedures for the steps you feel necessary to evaluate a person. Always remember that each person is a valuable asset and it is up to the people in charge to determine if a person will help or hurt the place where they work.

This book is written to assist businesses, Churches, and Organizations how to be successful. My many experiences and my relationship with God is the reason for writing this book to assist others to being successful.

NOTE: *Additional information about examples can be found in my life story book*

Thirteen books I have written. They will all soon also be in LuLu publications.

The following is a briefing of the books`.

1. **_Is There A God? How Do You Know (2016)_**

This is my life story from 1936 (age 4) to 2017 age 85) Disabled veteran April 9, 1951 overseas, world traveler Sunday School teacher and story teller. Owned businesses and Management for Corporations. Married raised 6 children and much more.

2. Adventurous Life Worth Living (2017)

This is the same book as **_Is There A God? How Do You Know_** with a change of title. Both books has been endorsed by Mary Eisenhower (President Eisenhower's Granddaughter), Dr. Robert Jeffress, Pastor First Dallas Baptist Church and Pastor Steve Stroope, Pastor Lake Pointe Baptist Church.

3. A Donkey Christmas in color (2017)

This is the Christmas Story as if the Donkey told the story from when he was first selected by Joseph. This is the donkey that carried Mary to give birth to Jesus in Bethlehem as told in the Bible. It is written for children to understand the birth of Jesus and has color pictures.

4. **Donkey Christmas Story in color (2018)**

This book is the same story as number 3 with a different title.

5. I Spent Christmas With Jesus (2018)

Could you image a young boy being lost the day before Christmas Eve in a major snow storm and found the day after Christmas. His story is that he was found and saved by a man who he said was Jesus Christ. At the request of his pastor he gave his story as a testimony and the pastor's message at church. Could this really happen?

6. Mystery in The Forest (2017)

This book is about some of the mysterious stories that can come from the forest. This is a factious story that could be from real life. The story will challenge the reader in their life with what happen to these people. You will meet two families who experience some unusual circumstances, including involvement of unusual stories within the forest. One person who almost lost his family, but what happen in the forest saved his marriage. The mysteries in the forest will be an unusual part of the story that will cause you to think about yourself and others.

7. Miracle Dream Teacher (2017)

This is a story about a young boy and girl that did not live near each other and the boy in grade school had failing grade in math, English and art. One night when both were asleep they met for the first time in a dream. The girl started to help the boy with his school work in the dream both of them were having. As the story moves forward it has an amazing story in court and a big surprise ending.

8. Youth Restoring America (2018)

This is a story of how American Students can assist to resolve some of American Government problems. The goal of this educational addition is to involve our youth in identifying problems in our government that our founding fathers already provided corrections. These young students researched and gave answers to government officials.

9. Mystery of the Bells (2018)

Mystery of the bells is a story of church bells ring with no one doing it. Also a story of the live of a Pastor of the church and a boy having their lives saved by animals and the unbelievable story being given as a sermon in the church with again the bells ringing without anyone to ring them. A surprise ending.

10. **Simple Formula for Successful Business and Churches (2019)**

This book has 19 examples of how to be successful in business and also it applies to all churches.

11. **Can America Be Saved (2019**

The United States of America was first found in 1492 and our Founding Fathers provided the laws and duties with the help of God to be different than the rest of the world. This book provides what changes are necessary to return America back to the original laws and regulations, including remembering this country was founded as a Christian Nation.

12. American History into Today (2019)

This book has some of the history and can be used in addition to the book number 11 "CAN AMERICA BE SAVED"

13. The Boy The Man and the Sea_2019

An adventure story on board a ship where a 11 year old boy and a 13 year old girl spent their Spring Break working on the ship. Both were not known to be on board the ship until it left its port. An amazing story with a very special surprise ending.

www.ingramcontent.com/pod-product-compliance
Lightning Source LLC
Chambersburg PA
CBHW021506210526
45463CB00002B/910